CANOE COUNTRY REFLECTIONS

W hen the first white man arrived to North America, he looked out over the land and he called it "a pristine, untouched wilderness." That's got to be the greatest compliment that anybody could pay to the native people, who have lived here for thousands of years. It's still possible to catch a glimpse of what that wilderness used to be. And I think the best way to do that is in a canoe: the most beautiful and functional craft ever created.

—BILL MASON, a man of many talents who captured North American hearts with films and books that shared his love for the canoe and concern for the environment.

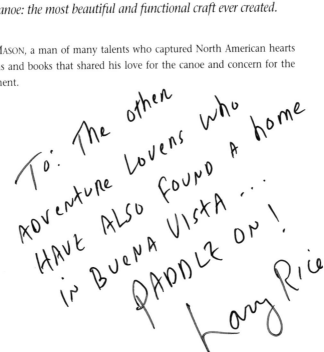

To: The other Adventure Lovers who have also found a home in Buena Vista... PADDLE ON!

Larry Rice

From *Waterwalker* by Bill Mason: a video distributed by NorthWord Press, Inc. Minocqua, WI.

Canoe Country Reflections

Reflections of the Wilderness Series

by

LARRY RICE

Photographs by Larry Rice

ICS BOOKS, INC.
Merrillville, Indiana

Canoe Country Reflections

Dedication

This book is dedicated to my father. I never could tempt him into a canoe—golf was his sport. But his unflagging encouragement whenever I set off into the outback will be sorely missed.

Published by:
ICS Books, Inc.
1370 E. 86th Place
Merrillville, IN 46410
800-541-7323

Co-Published in Canada by:
Vanwell Publishing LTD.
1 Northrup Crescent, P.O. Box 2131,
St Catharines, Ontario L2M 6P5
800-661-6136

Library of Congress Cataloging-in-Publication Data

Rice, Larry, 1950–
    Canoe country reflections / written by Larry Rice ; photographs by Larry Rice.
        p. cm. — (Reflections of the wilderness)
    Includes index.
    ISBN 0-934802-85-8 : $11.99
    1. Canoes and canoeing—North America—Guidebooks. 2. North America—Guidebooks. I. Title. II. Series.
GV776.05.R53 1993
797.1'22'09795—dc20
                                        93-26670
                                            CIP

Table of Contents

Preface

I remember my first canoe trip as if it were yesterday: twenty-five years later I can laugh about it. My two pals and I were seniors in a suburban Chicago high school—this was going to be our last (and first!) excellent adventure together before heading off to college. Minnesota's million-acre Boundary Waters Canoe Area seemed a good place to explore for a week. Here we'd find North Woods, black bears, bald eagles and "sky-blue waters" right out of one of those beer commercials. To be sure, all that good stuff was there. So were a few other things: mosquitoes (zillions of them, made more noticeable because *one of us forgot the tent*) and thumb-sized leeches that fastened to our butts when we dared to go skinny-dipping. Plus how could I ever forget our borrowed 18 1/2-foot canoe? I swear the shiny metallic beast weighed the same as I did back then—138 pounds dripping wet.

But despite the killer portages, the bug bites, our own goofiness, we persevered. And I'm glad we stayed. There were beautiful sunsets to ponder, fish to catch, countryside so spectacular that it took our breath away. My two buddies have never stepped foot in a canoe since then, but I hear they're still boring their kids about that singular adventure.

And me? I now own several canoes—solo and tandem, Kevlar and ABS—and I take great pleasure in paddling them as often as I can. A lot of things have changed in the past quarter-century, but the essence of paddlesport is as old as humankind itself. Plop a person in a canoe and an elemental desire to seek out watery horizons remains. Which gets me to thinking: People change too. Maybe I'll ask my citified friends if they want to join me in a Boundary Waters reunion next year.

Acknowledgments

My sincere thanks to the folks at *Canoe* magazine for finding room over the years for my articles and for keeping me busy at the writing craft. And thanks to Judy Bradford, my wife, trip companion, best friend, and ruthless live-in editor.

Introduction

It is first light and a heavy dew lies on the ground. You prop yourself up on your elbows and look around your river camp. The sky is pink and red as the sun crests the tree line, which is just beginning to show a tinge of green. A spindly legged great blue heron walks the edge of a sandbar, searching the shallows for frogs and small fish. A beaver swims lazily by, headed home to its bank burrow, its work finished for the night.

Soon, you sit tending the stove, recounting yesterday's progress in your notebook. Yawns penetrate the stillness as camp comes alive. Your friends appear from inside the tent, from under an overturned canoe. You smile at their disheveled appearance and tell them breakfast is ready. An appreciative grunt means they are as hungry as you.

Then it's back on the water, away from the car, away from the phone, riding the currents under your own power to another campsite, just as the American Indian, the voyageur, the missionary did before. You savor the joy of accomplishment, of finding a different reality from your work-a-day world.

ℴ

Canoes are marvelous chariots that can take you to remote and exciting places; however, one of the beauties of paddlesport is that it doesn't take vast acreages or faraway exotic places to feel like you're really in the wilderness. Chances are there's a wild, free-flowing river or secluded lake within a day's drive of your home.

Waterways have their own character and personality. Here, in North America, we are indeed fortunate. We have rivers that express every disposition imaginable, from high-thrills big water to relaxing voyages down meandering streams. We have lakes that you can cross in a half-hour with the kids and others that require months and a major expedition. Whether it's simply a break from the daily grind you're after, or whether it's stunning geological formations, wildlife, magnificent scenery, good fishing, or demanding white water, a paddle trip is the best way I know to seek it out.

If there is a message in this book of words and photographs, it is to reflect on the beauty, wonder, and yes, magic, of the *paddling experience*. Self-propelled and self-sufficient travel is a journey of both the body and the soul.

CHAPTER 1

Mountain West

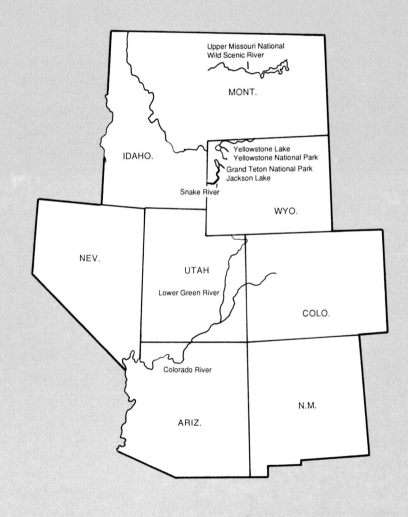

UPPER MISSOURI NATIONAL WILD AND SCENIC RIVER, MONTANA

Feel the mighty river pulse beneath your hull. Carved through the heart of the northern Great Plains, the Upper Missouri is cowboy country at its best: rugged, empty, and wholly undeveloped. Furrowed prairie sprawls forever in every direction.

After dinner, with camp chores done and a hot drink in hand, it's time to take turns reading passages out loud from the journals of Captains Meriwether Lewis and William Clark, leaders of one of the most skillfully managed expeditions in the history of North

American explorations. Called the Voyage of Discovery, the expedition lasted twenty-eight months from 1804 to 1806 and covered eight thousand miles, between the mouth of the Missouri River at St. Louis and the Pacific outlet of the Columbia River. Their campsites are scattered along the 150-mile stretch of wild and scenic river, from Fort Benton to Robinson Bridge. The Upper Missouri is little changed from when they passed beside it.

Time and elements have erased most signs of settlers along the river, but on occasion the remains of a homestead shack or cabin rears up from a grassy bench. Dating back to the early 1900s, these remnant frame-and-log dwellings give testimony to those who tried to eke out a living along the Upper Missouri. As you wander through the weathered shells, inspecting the bare cupboards, cast-iron stoves, old steamer trunks, rickety bed frames, and crumbling stone fireplaces, it's easy to think of dreams that were not to be—of someone's silent, broken memories.

(Above) Bighorn sheep are frequently spotted while floating the Upper Missouri. A single dominant ram, its massive amber-colored horns forming almost a full curl, holds reign over a pair of underling rams and an assorted flock of ewes, yearlings, and lambs. In 1805, Captain Lewis recorded seeing a large herd of bighorns in nearly the identical location. Here, complete with spelling errors, is his journal entry: "They feed on grass but principally on the arromatic herbs which grow on the clifts and inaccessible hights which they usually frequent. the places they ge[ne]rally celect to lodg is the cranies or c[r]evices of the rocks in the faces of inacessable precepices, where the wolf nor bear can reach them and where indeed man himself would in many instancies find a smiliar deficiency; yet these anamals bound from rock to rock and stand apparently in the most careless manner on the sides of precipices of many hundred feet. they are very shye and are quick of both sent and sight."

(Left) Break camp and ferry across the river for one more hike before you depart. Your objective will be to peer through the Eye of the Needle, an unusual sandstone arch perched on a two-hundred-foot cliff directly over the river. Framed through the eye is a landscape without walls, a hundred square miles of northern Great Plains prairie through which the tranquil Missouri flows.

Yellowstone Lake's dimensions are impressive: it is the largest high-mountain lake in the lower 48 States. Covering 139 square miles, it rests at an elevation of 7,733 feet. It is also home to powerful winds. Surrounding high mountains and plateaus create sweeping downdrafts that blast across the wide basin. But there are also calm days. Ferdinand V. Hayden, leader of expeditions to Yellowstone in the past century, described the lake as "a vast sheet of quiet water, of a most delicate ultramarine hue, one of the most beautiful scenes I have ever beheld. Such a vision is worth a lifetime."

Wet snow falls during the night, piling around the tents and covering the boats in a white shroud. You stick your head out the door and recoil from the cold. The thermometer reads just ten degrees—and it's mid-September! Burrowing deeper into your sleeping bag, you close your eyes and wait for morning. A place of fall moods and abrupt changes, Yellowstone Lake has thrown you another curve.

There are several backcountry lakeshore campsites on Jackson Lake; nothing else you can do in Teton Park will get you so quickly and easily into the peace of a wilderness setting. This is especially so in autumn, when the aspen and cottonwood trees attain their most brilliant yellow hues, and when the high-pitched bugles of bull elk ring across the water on a frosty night.

A solid layer of clouds hangs like a cheerless blanket above your island camp. You have coffee and instant oatmeal and pack the canoes. In summer, Jackson Lake is lousy with motorboats. But now it seems as though you have the entire park to your-selves. In an hour or so the gray scud begins to lift. Suddenly, Mount Moran appears. Its bare-rock summit towers overhead, while a puffy ribbon of clouds climbs steadily up its base.

Drifting quietly along the Snake River, it's possible to obtain new and unusual views of the Grand Tetons, a congregation of blue-gray pyramids soaring more than a mile above the sagebrush flats. Nathaniel P. Langford, a member of the Washburn Yellowstone Expedition of 1870, first saw the three Tetons in the clear light of the midday sun. In his diary, he wrote: "Some member of our party has asked what is the meaning of the word `Teton' given to these mountains. Lieutenant Doane says it is a French word signifying `Woman's Breast,' and that it was given to these mountains by the early French explorers, because of their peculiar shape. I think that the man who gave them this name must have seen them from a great distance; for as we approach them, the graceful curvilinear lines which obtained for them this delicate appellation appear angular and ragged. He indeed must have been of a most susceptible nature, and, I would fain believe, long a dweller amid these solitudes, who could trace in these cold and barren peaks any resemblance to the gentle bosom of woman."

LOWER GREEN RIVER, UTAH

(Above) The boats are loaded and you shove off into the swirling, silty current. Your launch site at Green River State Park quickly fades behind. Within minutes you are alone in a high desert plateau of windswept flats, long-abandoned ranches, and phantasmagoric canyons—places that bend the mind as you drift through them and into Canyonlands National Park. Major John Wesley Powell, one of America's most famous explorer-scientists, charted this country 125 years ago, but even he only skimmed the surface. Today, still plenty of discoveries remain. Labyrinth Canyon, Stillwater Canyon, the Maze, the Dollhouse, and the Confluence are just a few of the geologic oddities that await you before trip's end.

(Right, facing page) Compared to the immensity of the place, you feel insignificant, Lilliputians and their boats, camped on an acre-sized mound of sand at the base of a precipitous cliff. Powell must have been similarly affected. When passing through this section during his 1869 expedition, he wrote: "In many places the walls, which rise from the water's edge, are overhanging on either side. The stream is still quiet, and we glide along through a strange, weird, grand region."

Now, with your own voyage nearly over, you might recall a passage written by Julius Stone, a wealthy adventurer who made a dream-of-a-lifetime trip down the Green and Colorado rivers in 1909: "The scene near the mouth of the Green River, both in the canyon and from the top of the walls, is varied, impressive, and commanding. Some day, perhaps, surfeited globetrotters, after having tired of the commonplace scenery and flabby diversions in foreign lands, will learn what a wonderful region here awaits them."

CHAPTER 2

North Central

Voyageurs National Park

Isle Royale
National Park

L. SUPERIOR

MICHIGAN (U.P.)

L. HURON

N.D.

Sylvania
Recreation
Area

MINN.

Bois Brule River

WIS.

Flambeau River

L. MICHIGAN

MICH.

Kickapoo River

Horicon Marsh

L. ERIE

S.D.

Upper Iowa River

Niobrara River

IOWA.

OHIO.

NEB.

ILL.

IND.

Middle Fork of the
Vermilion River

Blue River

ISLE ROYALE NATIONAL PARK, LAKE SUPERIOR, MICHIGAN

Camp is pitched on a small island just offshore of Isle Royale, fifteen miles from the nearest mainland. Daylight is long in June, and there's still time to take an evening paddle on the cold northern waters of Lake Superior. The night is quiet and still with promise of bright stars and possibly even an aurora. No other boats, no artificial noises, no blemishes anywhere mar the overwhelming sensation of being on a seascape that is elemental wilderness at its best.

Ever since the first portage at McCargoe Cove, you've been following the same trail the Chippewas once used to cut across the island from north to south. This Indian Portage Trail, as it is now called, allowed them to avoid paddling their canoes on the often treacherous Lake Superior when traveling from one fishing and hunting camp to another. The track is rocky and several miles long, sometimes going high on an escarpment, sometimes low past beaver dams and lodges. Eighteenth-century voyageurs, small but incredibly tough men, regularly carried their heavy birchbark canoes *and two 90-pound packs* on trails such as these—and jogged doing it! By contrast, the majority of modern-day voyageurs, with their "ultra-light" outfits, make two carries across the portage and even then find themselves huffing through the woods.

A gauze of morning mist brushes the surface of Chickenbone Lake in the island's interior. The canoes wait patiently to carry you toward the next campsite—over one more ridge then back onto the openness of Lake Superior.

A moose peeks through the shrubs near shore. The young bull, his antlers covered with soft velvet, takes a bold step into the open, looks your way, then retreats to heavy cover.

You leave Anderson Bay at dawn—a figurative term, as there is no sunrise. Your world is wrapped in ethereal grayness. You can see the tip of your boat and maybe fifty feet of dark, oily water ahead; Rainy Lake's long, spacious vistas will have to wait for later. Strangely, the limited visibility offers good opportunities to become acquainted with some of the area's rich and varied fauna. Flocks of mergansers and gulls perch resignedly on water-lapped rock slabs. The disembodied voices of Canada geese and loons add an otherworldliness to the scene. A river otter swims so close that your boat slices over its bubbles when it submerges.

BOIS BRULE RIVER,
BRULE RIVER STATE FOREST, WISCONSIN

You huddle under the boughs of a white pine, waiting for the June rain to stop. You are eager to paddle the May Ledges, the last major set of rapids on the Bois Brule before it empties into the southwest corner of Lake Superior. Upsets and dunkings are the rule, not the exception, on this turbulent stretch of boulder- and ledge-strewn water. Sigurd F. Olson, the renowned naturalist and writer, may have never canoed the Brule, but he certainly knew something about running white water after living in the north woods all his life. "Rapids are a challenge. Dangerous though they may be, no one who has known the canoe trails of the

north does not love their thunder and rush of them. No man who has portaged around white water, studied the swirls, the smooth slick sweeps and the V's that point their way above the breaks, has not wondered if he should try. Is there any suspense that quite compares with that moment of commitment when the canoe then is taken by its unseen power? Rapids can be run in larger craft, but it is in a canoe that one really feels the river and the power of it."

By the time you reach Glimmerglass Lake, a small and shallow cove connected to Clark Lake, the sun has crested the trees and is radiating welcome warmth. Wool mittens, stocking hats, and pile jackets are peeled off as the temperature rockets up from the 20s to the mid-40s. Silently, you enter the narrow channel leading into Glimmerglass, curious to see what lies beyond. A small flock of hooded mergansers are near the opposite shore, the males bobbing their black-and-white crested heads in courtship displays. And not far away, a pair of mallards swim slowly off, tense upon seeing you. Not wanting to frighten them, you leave. There are still many other lakes to explore in the coming days.

FLAMBEAU RIVER,
FLAMBEAU RIVER STATE FOREST, WISCONSIN

Aldo Leopold (1887—1948) was a man of many talents: writer, philosopher, forester, professor, wildlife manager. He is perhaps best remembered for his later years in central Wisconsin, the scene of his classic literary work, *A Sand County Almanac*. When Leopold wanted a quick escape "from too much modernity," he would seek relaxation on an undeveloped Wisconsin river—"a sanctuary for the primitive art of wilderness travel, especially canoeing." A free-running, fifty-mile section of the Flambeau River was his favorite. He wrote, "In a few spots [the Flambeau] has hardly changed since Paul Bunyan's day; at early dawn one can still hear it singing in the wilderness. . . ."

Ease down the narrow, shaded stream. Its natural rhythms help you forget about the porkbarrel project that nearly destroyed this place. The valley is verdant and peaceful, the perfect backdrop for a slow-paced paddle on a warm June day. Although it is Saturday, you see no one, not even an angler casting for smallmouth bass, trout, or northern pike. About one thousand canoes ply the Kickapoo each week during the peak season, but severe thunderstorms forecasted for the weekend may have scared everyone away. Having expected a crowd, you embrace the solitude instead.

Each fall, Horicon Marsh, in east-central Wisconsin, hosts one of the grandest wildlife spectacles in the nation when upwards of one hundred thousand Canada geese congregate here during their southward migration. What draws canoeists to Horicon is the same thing that attracts the honkers year after year: the largest freshwater cattail

marsh in the United States, a 31,000-acre expanse known locally as the "Everglades of the North." There is the same shallow water. There are the green mats of aquatic plant life. There are the birds. And there are the clouds, big fat cumuli drifting like ghostly sailing ships over the watery prairie.

UPPER IOWA RIVER, IOWA

A brilliant flash of lightning sears the night sky. A rolling kettle-drum boom follows immediately. "Take cover!" someone yells, and you dive headlong into the tents. As the flaps zip shut, a powerful gust of wind sweeps through the valley. Trees shake and shudder; branches bend and break. Rain begins to fall in torrents, pelting the tents without letup. One shelter lifts slightly off the ground and then settles back down. In other words, good fun.

The Upper Iowa meanders for 135 miles from its source near LeRoy, Minnesota, to its mouth at New Albin, Iowa, where it empties into the mighty Mississippi. Soon you'll have your first taste of the unusual geological formations that make the Upper Iowa unique among Midwestern streams. At a U-shaped bend, you nearly crash into a sheer limestone palisade that looms one hundred feet overhead. Nearby, pillars of chimney, pulpit, and steamboat rocks stand apart from the cliff. You wonder when one last toppled into the river.

At first the Niobrara is not much more than a creek, but by the time it reaches north-central Nebraska's Sandhills, an expanse of rolling grass-covered dunes where cattle and antelope far outnumber people, the creek has grown into a fair-sized canoeable river. Here, nestled in a tree-lined Great Plains valley, the Niobrara is an American heartland treasure. Six different ecological zones intersect along the river, from Rocky Mountain pine forests to tall grass prairies. And enjoying these diverse habitats are fauna representative of both the East and West—sort of a biological United Nations. You'll not find a prettier prairie stream.

It is nearly dark when you arrive at your campsite. From here it is only a short hike to Smith Falls, the highest waterfall in Nebraska. Like a fleecy bridal veil, the spring-fed stream plunges seventy feet over a cliff into a mossy pool, then tumbles toward the Niobrara below.

From a paddler's standpoint, the Middle Fork of the Vermilion, Illinois' sole National Scenic River, is narrow and intimate, with numerous bends and elbows, boulder riffles, deep pools, and sand-and-gravel bars. Except for the sound of birds and maybe the distant drone of a farm tractor, the atmosphere is bucolic and serene. The rugged banks are heavily wooded with a mosaic of deciduous trees, interrupted in places by tall, steep bluffs sparsely covered with eastern red cedars. Occasional small hillside prairies serve to remind you of Illinois' heritage as a prairie state.

BLUE RIVER, INDIANA

The current is brisk, despite the river's gentle gradient. You ease downstream under a tunnel of sycamores, beech, hickories, and maples—'coon and 'possum bottomlands typical of southern Indiana. Not so typical are the river's limestone walls: most are cloaked with trees, shrubs, and vines, but at the more accessible cliffs it's worth stopping to examine ice-cold springs that gush out of small caves. As the day wears on, you see only a few other canoeists, most of them students on break from nearby universities. The serenity aids in your quest for wildlife. A subtle movement in the forest catches the eyes. A white-tailed deer, alert for signs of danger, emerges from the underbrush. Assured that all is safe, the doe makes a strange bleating sound. Two spotted fawns, quavering on wobbly legs, come out of hiding then disappear back into the uninviting growth of nettles and poison ivy.

CHAPTER 3

South Central

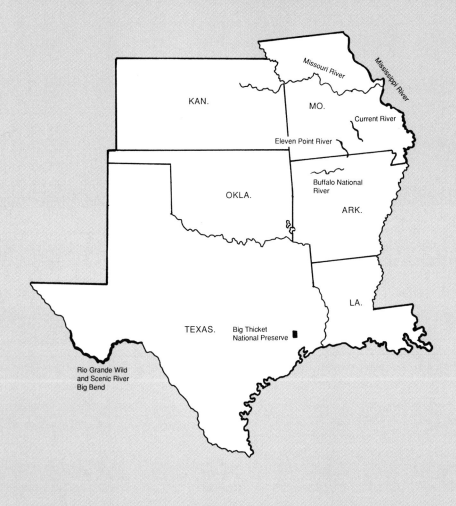

Camp comes alive as you greet the sunrise. Naked bodies appear from under the overturned canoes, others tumble out from inside walled canvas tents. You smile as you recognize their grizzled faces. In a few minutes there are twenty men—young and old, bearded and whiskered, boisterous and quiet—getting ready for another long day of paddling to reach the big rendezvous. It has been an eventful journey from the Rocky Mountains, but a journey done well.

Throughout their travels, the voyageurs have seen the effects of modern man on the Mississippi and its tributaries, but nowhere is it as apparent as when approaching St. Louis. The roar of low-flying jet aircraft, interstate highway bridges, and intense river-side development comes first, followed by mile after mile of powerful tugs pushing barges laden with coal, rock, and grain. ⌐Midmorning on May 30, five weeks and 1,200 miles after launching their heavily laden canoes into the South Platte River out-side of Denver, the tanned and travel-hardened buckskinners arrive at the Gateway to the West Arch, a small park and museum administered by the National Park Service in the center of the city. Inside the museum are exhibits explaining the Lewis and Clark

expedition, the Louisiana Purchase, and other historical events that made the St. Louis area the meeting ground of early explorers. Outside, in the sweltering heat, among a backdrop of restored paddle-wheeler cruise boats and a floating McDonald's and Burger King, crowds of school groups and tourists are delighted to encounter reincarnations of the early French fur traders.

It's just another step on the beat for a National Park Service river ranger. She works the Ozark National Scenic Riverway—a hundred miles of the Current River and thirty-four miles of its main tributary, the Jacks Fork. Together, these two rivers form one of the Midwest's most splendid waterways, and one of the most heavily canoed rivers in the United States. More than twelve million people live within a day's drive. From late spring through Labor Day, especially on weekends, the park bulges at the seams with those seeking the Great Outdoors.

ELEVEN POINT RIVER, MISSOURI

The Eleven Point flows southeasterly through the Ozarks of southern Missouri. With clear water, forested banks, countless springs, and abundant wildlife, the river looks much the same today as it did a hundred years ago. Because of these special qualities, a forty-four mile section of the Eleven Point was designated a National Scenic River in 1968. There are many ways to become familiar with the river, but perhaps a two- to three-day trip, in mid-March to April, is best. During this period, canoe traffic is extremely light, bugs are no problem, and water levels are generally superb. Paddling the Eleven Point is enjoyable other months, of course, but there's nothing like spring when the trees and wildflowers are in bloom and wild turkeys are gobbling in the woods.

Around lunchtime you pull over near Big Bluff, the tallest limestone cliff in the Ozarks at more than five hundred feet high. During the break, there's time to study the map and review the park brochure. In 1972, the Buffalo became this country's first National River, a designation providing even more protection than that afforded under the National Wild and Scenic Rivers System. Managed by the National Park Service, the Buffalo is one of the longest stretches of free-flowing water in the lower 48 states. A sobering thought when you stop to consider how many other rivers would be as wild and free-flowing if they weren't diverted or dammed.

A few miles downstream of Big Bluff, a flat rock ledge signals the take-out for the trail to Hemmed-in-Hollow. The scramble up a narrow, dead end canyon leads you to a two-hundred-foot free-leaping waterfall, the highest of its kind between the Southern Appalachians and the Rockies.

On the extreme eastern edge of Texas is a crazy quilt of blackwater bayous, swamps, and savannahs called the Big Thicket. Once it covered more than three million acres; now only about 300,000 scattered acres remain. An exploration of the Thicket takes you into another world. The cypress sloughs and oxbow lakes along the slow-moving Upper Neches River is a dim and spooky place, mostly the realm of birds, gators, river otters, razorback hogs, and snakes—lots of snakes. Spanish moss drips from gnarled, moss-covered limbs; suspended from the branches are swathes of creepers and wild grape vines as thick as your wrist. Skeletons of trees add to the gloom.

RIO GRANDE WILD AND SCENIC RIVER
BIG BEND, TEXAS

You push off from the sandy bank and are grabbed by the strong current. A short time later you are flushed into what is the first of many canyons to come. The remoteness of the Rio Grande's Lower Canyons, with few access roads and intermittent Class II-III rapids, requires experience in both wilderness skills and river running. Because a serious accident on this stretch of river could result in a life-threatening situation, a member of the Texas Explorers Club issues this simple, strict directive: "Don't break no legs!"

The miles pass quickly as paddles work in unison with the river's flow. After a quick lunch, you shoot into the corridor of Big Canyon. The narrow chasm, with its unclimbable walls and lively rapids, is a welcome diversion from the monotonous desert plains that you left behind.

A cold, faint starlight provides just enough illumination to see your companions still stretched out in sleeping bags on the sandbar nearby. Bats flicker past, and a sheer cliff face, dark and foreboding, leans drunkenly overhead. It's still too dark to make out the river, but its endless gurgles and splashes is music to your ears.

RIO GRANDE, COLORADO CANYON,
BIG BEND, TEXAS

You and your partner have discussed the run for a half-hour and are too anxious to wait any longer. Kneeling low in the canoe, you paddle into the current and point

the bow downstream, lining up on a boulder that marks the correct chute. Things, however, appear markedly different from a canoe seat than they do on shore. Slightly off-course, you wallow through two standing waves before being torpedoed by a killer haystack. Your partner leans out to brace but catches only foam-flecked air. Into the drink you go.

CHAPTER 4

The Southeast

OKEFENOKEE NATIONAL WILDLIFE REFUGE, GEORGIA

More than nine-tenths of the Okefenokee Swamp is included in the Okefeno-kee National Wildlife Refuge, a remote tangle of forest and river channels guaranteed to make you feel like the Last Canoeist on Earth. As you pass through Minnie's Lake, a narrow pond really, where cypress trees with exposed roots the size of fire hoses rise upward from the inky water, the reality of the swamp is in sharp contrast from the mysterious and menacing myth portrayed in movies and books. Thoreau wrote that "hope and the future for me are not in lawns and cultivated fields, not in towns and cities, but in the impervious and quaking swamps . . . that was the jewel which dazzled me." You're dazzled too as you paddle out into the sun.

John "Crawfish" Crawford stands in the stern of his canoe as soon as you're free from overhanging trees. The Okefenokee guide has traded his paddle for a long bamboo pole to propel the boat along the "prairie" channel. Crawfish points out catbirds and yellowthroats and phoebes hiding in the shrubbery, and is familiar with every botanical specimen along the way. At intervals, you stop to examine unusual plants, such as the carnivorous sundew with its sticky, long wands; and signs of animals, such as the small, dome-shaped grassy nests of the rarely seen water rat. You don't need a guide to canoe the Okefenokee, but these are things you're likely to pass right over when visiting on your own.

(*Above*) The atmosphere is cathedral-like, hushed and reverent. As still as glass, the rain-swollen river creates a reflection so deep and intense that while paddling it's hard to distinguish the reality from the image of what lies ahead. Spanish moss hangs in clusters from the branches and also—in the water—from upside-down red-blossomed trees. The canoe is a stereoscopic picture of itself until a paddle blade slices the water and the likeness shatters and dissolves.

(*Left, facing page*) Thanks to Stephen Foster, writer of America's most hummable songs, the Suwannee River is famous. In 1851, when Foster composed "Old Folks at Home" (better known as "Way Down Upon the Suwannee River"), the Suwannee ran through wild, uncultivated country with only a few plantations scattered along its length. This part of the South has been through some drastic changes since then, but much of the beauty and wildness of the Suwannee remain. Follow the Suwannee's twists and turns from Fargo, Georgia, near the edge of the Okefenokee, into Florida. You'll learn that this (pardon the pun) is still a river worth singing about.

If any cockiness exists about your ability as a paddler, it can be easily obliterated after only a few minutes on the rambunctious Nantahala River just outside of Great Smoky Mountains National Park. Author Robert Kimber writes, "I recall one fellow who had just run his first Class III rapid exclaiming, 'Wow, that was almost as good as sex.'" That's something you'll have to decide for yourself.

CHAPTER 5

The Northeast

(*Above*) Paddling stern in the lead canoe, Alexandra weaves through light rapids. She alternates between standing and sitting as she snubs over shallow riffles with her twelve-foot spruce setting pole, then switches back to a paddle. Her style is graceful. She makes long, fluid throws and recoveries—a ballet on the water.

(*Left, facing page*) It is early October and the maples are riotous with color. The river is low, but not too shallow to run. You and six others, all new to the river, cluster at the water's edge and listen intently to your guides, Garrett and Alexandra Conover, for in a few minutes you will embark on a five-day trip down the Allagash Wilderness Waterway in northern Maine. Canoeing the Allagash is only one reason you are here. The other is to experience the Conovers' special approach to wilderness travel. You will be traveling in much the same fashion as Maine guides and trappers of a century ago, relying mostly on traditional, hand-made equipment, including beautifully crafted 18½-foot wood-and-canvas canoes.

The next few days on the river are both leisurely and moderately challenging. You go slowly, always searching ahead for the deep channels through shoals, pausing to observe animal tracks on the mudbars or a moose or a mink keeping pace on shore. In his book, *The Survival of the Bark Canoe,* John McPhee wrote: "Travel by canoe is not a necessity, and will nevermore be the most efficient way to get from one region to another, or even from one lake to another—anywhere. A canoe trip has become simply a rite of oneness with certain terrain, a diversion of the field, an act performed not because it is necessary, but because there is value in the act itself."

A wood fire and steaming cups of tea help chase away the chill on a rainy, windy day. As someone once said, "There is more to be learned in one day of discomfort than in a lifetime of apparent security."

CHAPTER 6

Canada

To the Ojibway, she was Kitchi Gummi, the Great Water, said to be the mother and mistress of all lakes. In Longfellow's *The Song of Hiawatha* she was the shining "Big-Sea-Water." And to the French, she was simply *Bourbon*, then *Supérieur*. In 1618, Etienne Brule was reportedly the first European to gaze upon Superior. He was impressed with "this body of water so large that one saw no land on either side." Soon after Brule came the voyageurs. It took them only two days with a crew of ten, to paddle a *canot du maitre* loaded with five tons of furs from the Pic River near Hattie Cove to the fur trading center of Michipicoten. By contrast, canoeists today plan on taking from a week to ten days, if they are lucky, to cover the one-hundred-dred-mile coastal route.

"Those who have never seen Superior get an inadequate, even inaccurate idea of hearing of it spoken as a lake. Though its waters are fresh and crystal, Superior is a sea. It breeds storms and rain and fog, like the sea. It is as cold in midsummer as the Atlantic. It is wild, masterful and dreaded." —THE REVEREND GEORGE GRANT, 1872

You trust your compass to guide you through the dense fog and mist so common on Superior. Only when you come across a long abandoned settlement near the mouth of a sluggish river can you pinpoint your exact location on the map. Each fall from 1905 to 1930, almost four hundred loggers and merchants lived in this desolate place called the Pukaskwa Depot. All that remains are dilapidated cabins and a weathered wooden cross that marks a grave—and all the ghosts that are still about.

You wake early to take advantage of the Indian summer weather and start out for Baie Fine, one of the remote arms of Georgian Bay that juts into the west end of the park. From O.S.A. Lake you portage into Muriel Lake, a small lake with red granite ridges and forested bluffs. The water here is shallow and thick with bright green weeds. After Muriel come three small lakes joined by short humpbacked trails and skinny channels that the beavers have clogged. The hard-packed dirt on the portages hint at heavy summer traffic, but the only traveler you see is a quick-moving mink.

A canoe trip into Killarney is only half-complete without scrambling up one of its white quartzite ridges. Paddle northeast on Killarney Lake and find a spot to begin your hike to the high country. A few hours later you'll be standing at the summit in the La Cloche Range, nearly twelve hundred feet up. The view is incredible. The forest below bristles with reds, yellows, golds, and greens. The lake shimmers about a quarter-mile away, and in the distance you can see green and limitless Georgian Bay.

SOPER RIVER, BAFFIN ISLAND, NORTHWEST TERRITORIES

The first thing you notice after the plane leaves is the silence, the profoundly deafening silence. You walk over to the river's edge to get a drink. The whispering gurgle of clean, clear water is reassuring and reaffirming. The soothing sound helps to clear from your head the blur of the past twenty-four hours. Your party of twelve met in Montreal. From there, at considerable expense, you flew to this spot thousands of miles from home, just to spend the next six days canoe tripping on a little-known white water river on a treeless island in the eastern Arctic. Some people might laugh at this folly. No matter. To you it all makes perfect sense, now that you are poised to paddle your way out.

Bull caribou watch you nervously from ridge lines and gravel bars, their curiosity a dangerous trait in a valley where Inuit hunters still roam. You catch a glimpse of an arctic hare, a grayish-white animal about the size of a jackrabbit, but in this land where roller coaster perspectives confuse the eye, it looks as large as a deer. There are ravens, Canada geese, Lapland longspurs, snow buntings, and soaring hawks. At every opportunity, Dr. Bob, the avid angler among the group, casts a line into chilly clear pools that give you vertigo when you stare over the gunwales into their depths. His diligence is awarded with several nice-sized Arctic char.

You climb the escarpment that looms over camp. As an aficionado of untamed, windswept places, you like what you see. Except for a thin mantle of richly hued and flowered tundra, punctuated by a few dwarf arctic willows all of six inches tall yet 150 years old, the countryside is barren and austere. It seems that the bones of the earth itself are there to see. The river creates a feeling of perpetual motion, a highway to the unknown.